CHICAGO

Text by
David Stockwell

Photos by
Karina Wang

ƎB
BONECHI

Project and editorial conception: Casa Editrice Bonechi
Publication Manager: Monica Bonechi
Picture research: Karina Wang. *Cover:* Manuela Ranfagni
Graphic design and make-up: Laura Settesoldi *and* Manuela Ranfagni. *Editing:* Simonetta Giorgi
Map page 44 by Stefano Benini

Text: David Stockwell
Text revision: Karina Wang

© Copyright
by Casa Editrice Bonechi Florence - Italy
E-mail:bonechi@bonechi.it

Printed in Italy by Centro Stampa Editoriale Bonechi.

The photographs from the Archives of Casa Editrice Bonechi *are by* Karina Wang.

Pages 4 and 5: © Chicago Historical Society.
Page 55: © The Art Institute of Chicago.
Page 60: courtesy of the Field Museum of Natural History, *Chicago.*
Pages 63 and 64 top: courtesy of The Adler Planetarium.
Pages 66 and 67: courtesy of the Museum of Science and Industry, *Chicago.*

ISBN 978-88-476-2520-4
www.bonechi.com

* * *

MILLENNIUM CITY

Once in a thousand years...a Chicago

A proud city of Irish- African- Polish- Italian- Chinese- Greek- Mexican- German- Thai-Jewish- Japanese- English. Fairly swarming with hyphenated Americans, yet not at all a melting pot. Rather a collection of neighborhoods, intact, comfortable, and welcoming. Chicago enters the twenty-first century proud of its heritage, proud of the hardships overcome and confident of its future as a World City of the first rank. But it was a long, often bumpy road.

More than three hundred years ago...

explorers moving from east to west across North America discovered the distance between the Checagou River and the Des Plaines River to be only a few thousand yards, easily portaged by travelers in canoes. The Checagou connected with the east coast via the Great Lakes; the Des Plaines with the Mississippi and the western rivers. The place was important, and so the Checagou Portage, named after a wild onion, became the town of Chicago.

In 1674, the explorers Marquette and Joliet passed this way. LaSalle came in 1682 and claimed all the land touched by the Mississippi and its tributaries for France. He named it "Louisiana," after King Louis XIV.

The first non-native settler, in 1779, was Jean-Baptiste Point DuSable, a black man from the Caribbean island of Hispaniola. He was a successful trader who built a cabin roughly where the original **Prudential Building** stands, took a Potowatomi bride, raised three children, and saw the birth of a grandchild before departing for Missouri in 1804.

Fort Dearborn was built in 1803 at the present south end of the Michigan Avenue Bridge, where a *bas relief* on the bridge tower recalls the Ft. Dearborn Massacre in 1812. The native Americans of the Midwest, led by the charismatic Shawnee chief, Tecumseh, had united with the English to make war against the fledgling United States.

Just six years later in 1818, Illinois was admitted to the Union as the twenty-first state. Chicago was in a period of slow but steady growth as enthusiastic settlers moved westward seeking cheap and fertile land. Speculators followed, making Chicago a typical "boom and bust" town. The linkage by water between the manufacturers of the East and the markets of the West was finally achieved in 1848, when the Illinois-Michigan Canal was completed. In 1860, **Abe Lincoln** was nominated for the presidency in Chicago, and by the end of the Civil War the city was almost as big as St. Louis. The Union Stockyards

Chicago lights up in the morning sun.

Chicago Timeline

Year	Event	Year	Event	Year	Event
1673	Discovery	1885	First Skyscraper	1943	Chicago's First Subway Opened
1779	Jean-Baptiste Point du Sable	1886	The Haymarket Riot	1955	Richard J. Daley Elected Mayor
1803-12	The First Fort Dearborn	1888	Jane Addams — Hull House	1956	Congress Expressway Opened
1818	Illinois Admitted to Statehood	1893	World's Columbian Exposition		— Renamed Dwight D. Eisenhower
1833	Incorporated as a Town	1900	Flow of Chicago River Reversed		Expressway January 10, 1964
1837	Incorporated as a City		Includes brief history of the Sanitary	1958	International Trade Fair Celebrates
1840	Free Schools Established		District of Greater Chicago and the		Opening of St. Lawrence Seaway
1848	Illinois & Michigan Canal		present Tunnel and Reservoir Project		— Queen Elizabeth's Visit
	Completed		(TARP).	1966	Civic Center Dedicated — December
1848	First City Hall in State Street	1903	Iroquois Theater Fire		27, 1976 Renamed the Richard J.
1855	Police Department Created	1907	First American Nobel Prize		Daley Center
1860	First National Political Convention		Winner in Science From University	1967	August 15 — Picasso Statue Unveiled
	— Abraham Lincoln Nominated		of Chicago		In Civic Center Plaza
1861-65	The Civil War	1908	Chicago Plan Published — First	1973	Sears Tower Completed
1865	Chicago Union Stock Yard Completed		Comprehensive Outline Offered To An	1976	Mayor Richard J. Daley Dies at 74
1867	The First Tunnel Under the Lake		American City	1983	Harold Washington is Elected Mayor
1868	Chicago Water Tower	1915	Eastland Disaster	1989	Richard M. Daley Elected Mayor
1871	The Great Fire	1927	Municipal Airport of Chicago	2004	Millennium Park Opened
1872	Montgomery Ward — First Mail-Order		(Midway) Opened	2008	Opening of the Modern Wing of the
	House	1933-34	A Century of Progress		Art Institute — November 4
1873	Chicago Public Library (CPL)	1942	December 2 — First Controlled		— Chicago citizen Barack Obama is
	Opened		Atomic Reaction		elected President of the United States.

Left: Chicago in 1832: Wolf Point. Lithograph from a drawing by George Davis. Creator: Rufus Blanchard.

Below: Rush Street Bridge on the turn of the Chicago River; ca. 1869. Photo by J. Carbutt.

opened in 1865, giving Chicago its character as "hog butcher to the world," and providing jobs for generations of immigrant workers.

The Great Chicago Fire

When fire swept through in 1871, the city had a population of 300,000. The blaze cleansed Chicago of its ramshakle slums, riverfront saloons, and wooden sidewalks. It also destroyed the graceful old homes and worthy commercial buildings, but the catastrophe created an opportunity unique among great cities to begin anew.

The late years of the century saw unparalleled growth for the City of Chicago despite a series of labor troubles, culminating in the notorious Haymarket Riot of 1885. That same year saw completion of the prototype of the modern skyscraper, the **Home Insurance Building**, designed by William LeBaron Jenny, towering all of *ten stories* above the intersection of Adams and LaSalle Streets. **The Rookery** opened the next year, eleven floors with six hundred offices, right across the street. It still stands, a monument to

designers Daniel Burnham and
John Root.

The Columbian Exposition

Enjoying a population of more
than a million in 1890, Chicago
was chosen to host the World's
Fair in 1892, celebrating the
four hundredth anniversary of
the discovery of America by
Christopher Columbus. The
Exposition put the city on the
international map with its **White
City** of modern architecture. One
of the noble buildings survives
today as the **Museum of Science
and Industry**.

The "Roaring Twenties"

In 1919, Alphonse Capone left
New York City and came to
Chicago. During the Prohibition
years, crime flourished, and
Chicago gained a reputation for
lawlessness, memories of which
still linger.

The "Bullish Nineties"

Happily, Michael Jordan has in
recent years bumped Alphonse to
second place as Chicago's best
known citizen. His graceful statue
can be admired just east of the
United Center.

The Atomic Age

A distinguished American of
Italian descent, Enrico Fermi,
succeeded in splitting the atom in
a squash court on the campus of
the University of Chicago in 1942.
An interesting sculpture by Henry
Moore marks the site on the Hyde
Park campus.
In 1955, Richard J. Daley was first
elected mayor. He served longer
than any other mayor, until his
death in 1976. In the mid-'60s, the
Civil Rights Movement centered
for a time on Chicago with the
visit of Martin Luther King in
1966 and the riots during the
Democratic Party Convention of
1968.
More recently, we have seen
the election of Jane Byrne, the
city's first woman chief executive
and Harold Washington, the
first African-American mayor.
Richard M. Daley, son of Richard J.,
became mayor in 1989.

*State Street looking north from Madison
Street; ca. 1905. Photo by Barnes-Crosby.*

*Following two pages:
A night view of Chicago.*

Chicago Today

Today's Chicago offers
sophisticated dining with almost
every international cuisine ably
represented. One can easily
spend $500 on dinner for two
(including a *nice* wine) at a four
star French restaurant. One can
also relish the world's very best
pizza and a glass of good beers
for about ten bucks. Four major
universities assure the continuing
presence of intelligent speakers
and other cultural activities. The
world class Chicago Symphony
Orchestra and Lyric Opera
crown the fall-winter season, and
a variety of summer festivals
explore almost all types of music
from classical to blues. Shopping,
theater, spectator sports, and a
great variety of tours by bus, boat,
and foot are here for the visitor.

WALT DISNEY

Walter Elias Disney was born in
Chicago on December 5, 1901.
His father, Elias Disney, was Irish-Ca-
nadian. His mother, Flora Disney, was
German-American. Walt was one of five
children, four boys and a girl. Walt early
became interested in drawing, selling
his first sketches to neighbors when he
was only seven years old. After the war,
Walt began his career as an adverti-
sing cartoonist. In 1920, he created and
marketed his first original animated
cartoons, and later perfected a new
method for combining live action and
animation.
Mickey Mouse was created in 1928,
and his talents were first used in a silent
cartoon entitled "Plane Crazy." However, Mickey made his screen debut
in "Steamboat Willie," the world's first
sound cartoon, which premiered at the
Colony Theatre in New York on November 18, 1928.
Disney died on December 15, 1966.

Facing page: View of the Loop looking from the south.

The Loop viewed from the west.

THE LOOP

The Loop was named for a rectangular section of elevated tracks which transport modern air conditioned Chicago Transit Authority electric trains around the central city and send them to neighborhoods and suburbs to the north, west, and south. "State Street, that great street" is the main street of the Loop. Formerly the retail shopping hub of the midwest, State Street still boasts the flagship store **Macy**, but the main shopping frenzy has moved to North Michigan Avenue.

The eastern edge of the Loop is Michigan Avenue where you'll find the splendid new **Symphony Center**, home of the elite Chicago Symphony Orchestra...and a little farther north is the exciting **Chicago Cultural Center**, at Washington Street, a must stop for visitors. This neoclassical palazzo offers free programs of dance, concerts, films, lectures, and exhibits as well as high quality memorabilia available at the *Visitor Information Center*.

Some Architectural Gems

Looming over the south end of State Street is the **Harold Washington Library Center**, the world's second largest public library. Only London's British Library is larger. A visitor then might stroll west on Jackson Boulevard to **The Monadnock Building** (53 West), once the world's tallest at sixteen stories, and further west to the **Board of Trade Building** (141 West) where a tour is available of the trading floor. North on LaSalle is **The Rookery**; check out the lobby, redesigned by Frank Lloyd Wright in 1905.

Then double back to Dearborn Street and turn left. Note the **Marquette Building** at 140 North with its *bas relief* sculptured facade over the entrance. Across the street at Monroe stands the **Inland Steel Building**. It is hard to believe this very modern structure was built in 1954. Across Dearborn at Madison soars the graceful curving profile of the **J. P. Morgan Chase Bank**. Turn left one block north on Washington and the **Richard J. Daley Center** (City Hall) is revealed behind the famous Picasso statue. Walk a block more to Randolph Street and turn left to view the interesting **James R. Thompson Center** (State of Illinois Building) designed by Helmut Jahn.

Other buildings of historical interest, and there are many, include the **Sullivan Building** at State and

Top left: Willis Tower overlooking Lake Michigan. Top right: Willis Tower from the south. Left: Perched 103 floors over the city streets, three newly added glass boxes on the west side of the Skydeck provide new thrills for visitors. Right: From the north branch of the Chicago River.

Madison designed by Louis Sullivan. The corner clock, a block north at Washington, the signature piece for **Macy**, formerly Marshall Field & Co., has been a rendezvous for generations of Chicagoans. "I'll meet you under the clock."

WILLIS TOWER

Known until July 2009 as the SEARS TOWER, the 108 story Willis Tower was the worlds tallest at the time of its completion in 1973 and remained so for 25 years. It is still the tallest building (1482 feet) in the United States. The new owners plan to transform it into the greenest skyscraper in the world.

It is surely Chicago's number one tourist attraction. The spectactular observation deck has its own entrance on Jackson Boulevard. Designed by architect Bruce Graham and engineer Fazlur Kahn of Skidmore, Owings, and Merrill, the same team which created the John Hancock Building, to be Sears national headquarters in 1974.

Above: The newest architecture along Randolph Street looking south over Millennium Park compliments the "Michigan Avenue Street Wall" with its century old buildings.

Preceding pages: Chicago's skyline seen from Lake Michigan.

Facing page: left: Tribune Tower and Wrigley Building. Right: Marina City by Goldberg (1967), One IBM Plaza by Mies van der Rohe (1971) and the Trump Tower by Skidmore, Owings & Merill (2009) - three neighbors along the Chicago River. Bottom left: Renzo Piano's (2009) new Modern Wing of the Art Institute blends in with Michigan Avenue's early 20th century architecture.

ARCHITECTURE AND BUILDINGS

"Make no little plans...
they have no magic to stir men's blood. Make big plans, aim high and hope... Remember that our sons and grandsons are going to do things that would stagger us."

Chicago's motto was expressed by an architect, Daniel Burnham, whose buildings stand today among the city's most cherished. He led the group of architects who designed **White City**, which became the site of the Columbian Exposition in 1890. Burnham was also the author of a "Plan of Chicago," issued in 1909, which, among many other things, assured the city of a lakefront unobstructed by buildings and other commercial development. Instead, beautiful parks: Lincoln, Grant, and Jackson line Lake Michigan from north to south.

Other architects whose work is highly visible in Chicago include Frank Lloyd Wright, Mies van der Rohe, and Helmut Jahn.

Wright was a designer, primarily of small buildings and family homes. The Chicago suburb of Oak Park, where Wright lived and worked, is the site of many Wright homes; the world famous **Robie House** stands proudly on the campus of the University of Chicago. His extraordinary genius is also in evidence in the lobby of **The Rookery** building in Chicago.

Mies came to the city in the nineteen thirties to head the Architecture Department at the Illinois Institute of Chicago. He is best known for the tall buildings he created himself and many others built in the 1960s and 1970s which were inspired by his carefully ordered style. These include the graceful **Lake Point Tower**, the **John Hancock Center**, and the **Willis Tower,** formerly Sears Tower. Prominent buildings designed by Mies himself include the apartment buildings at **900 and 910 Lake Shore Drive**, the **Kluczynski** and **Dirksen Federal Buildings** and the **IBM Building**. Mies is the author of the cryptic minimalist assertion, "Less is more."

Helmut Jahn is an architect of the 1980s and '90s. Glass is his medium, evidenced in the spectacular **One South Wacker Building**, the **Northwestern Atrium Center**, and the **James R. Thompson Center**. Jahn's most famous Chicago design, however, may very well prove to be the **United Airlines Terminal One Complex** at O'Hare Airport.

When Movies Played in Palaces...

The Chicago Theater, 125 N. State, has been restored to its former glory as a rococo performing palace. Back in 1921, it was called the "Wonder Theater of the World" by its owner Balaban & Katz, who built it at a cost of $4 million. Designed to showcase vaudeville performers as well as movies, the cavernous auditorium seats 3,800. The triumphal arch on the facade is supposed to resemble the Arc de Triomphe in Paris. Truly the architects, Rapp & Rapp, "made no little plans" here, and they were rewarded with many other commissions from the Paramount Theater chain across the country. The interior lobby, lush with crimson velours, is derived from the Chapelle Royale at Versailles. The Chicago now presents "family" entertainment. Two other ornate old movie houses, The Oriental and The Palace, now present large stage productions on Randolph Street:

The Rookery, 209 S. LaSalle, was designed by Burnham & Root and built in 1888 as "the most modern of office buildings." A central court is surmounted by a skylight. This area and the lobby were renovated in 1907 by Frank Lloyd Wright. The building offers a glimpse of downtown Chicago at the beginning of the 20th century.

Top left: The Chicago Theater.

Left and bottom: The Rookery.

Above left: Thompson Center lobby, designed by Helmut Jahn—a vast open space, impressive and popular with tourists, but almost impossible to air condition. The State of Illinois has its Chicago offices here. The exterior, paneled in salmon and blue is less successful.

Above right: the entrance to the Sullivan Building on State and Monroe Street, possibly the finest example of the intricate design work of Louis Sullivan.

Middle: J. P. Morgan Chase Bank—designed by Perkins & Will and built in 1969. This is Chicago's fourth highest building, made distinctive by its tapering walls.

Bottom: North Western Atrium Center—a very distinctive Helmut Jahn creation with cascading glass walls, exposed steel structure, and a traditional "Chicago Arch."

Above: Harold Washington Library Center.

Left: The Board of Trade Building guards the south end of LaSalle Street.

Below: The Board of Trade up close. The Federal Reserve Bank is at right.

Facing page: The Loop next to Grant Park and Millennium Park.

Left: "The Picasso" at State and Washington.

Above: "Flamingo" by Alexander Calder.

"THE PICASSO"

Controversy raged back in 1967 when a strange object was unveiled in the plaza at State and Washington just south of the Daley Center. Is it a bird...a horse...a baboon...a joke? Is this fellow Picasso "having us on" as the Brits say? Midwestern Chicago found its sophistication severely challenged. No guidelines were provided; the artist did not name or in any way identify the work. In time it became known simply as **"The Picasso,"** and the city has embraced it as a cherished symbol, along with the Art Institute Lions and Mrs. O'Leary's cow. Scholars now tend to agree the 162 ton Cor-Ten steel figure represents the head of a woman.

"FLAMINGO"

The American sculptor, Alexander Calder, created **"Flamingo"** in 1974. It nestles in a plaza on South Dearborn, flanked by two Mies van der Rohe federal office buildings. The contrast between the vivid "Calder orange" and the sparse black steel and glass of the buildings is interesting, and the 53 foot object invites pedestrians to walk around and through it, to get to know it well. In naming it, Calder said, "...it's sort of pink and has a long neck, so I called it 'Flamingo'."

21

Left top: "Agora" by Polish sculptor Magdalena Abakanowicz is a present from Warsaw, Poland, Sister City of Chicago. It was unveiled in November 2006 in the south west corner of Grant Park.

Left bottom: The contemporary Chicago sculptor, Richard Hunt, is represented here (160 North LaSalle) with a monumental Free Form Sculpture mounted between the 6th and 9th floors.

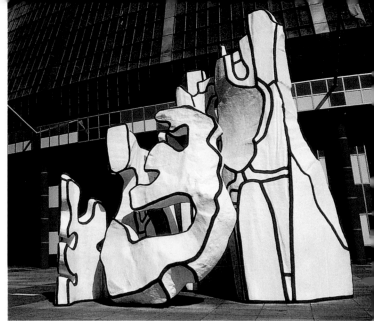

Right top: The whimsical "Monument à la Bête Débout" stands at Clark and Randolph and invites strollers to pass through. French sculptor, Jean Dubuffet, derived inspiration from the art of the insane and the art of children.

Right bottom: Joan Miro's Chicago stands across the street from "The Picasso". This slim-waisted lady is smaller but equally intriguing.

Below: 1974 was a banner year for major Loop sculpture. It brought "The Four Seasons," by Marc Chagall, to the plaza south of the J. P. Morgan Chase Bank. It is a 70 foot monolith, 10 feet wide and 14 feet tall, a mosaic of stone and glass fragments depicting six fantastic settings of Chicago.

Above: Sailboats approach the Michigan Avenue Bridge and the Trump Tower.

Facing page: The spring boat parade passing Marina Towers.

Following two pages: The river connects with Lake Michigan through locks. It separates the Loop on the south from the River North part of town.

THE CHICAGO RIVER

Here are two views of the annual spring boat parade. Hundreds of sailboats claim their marine right-of-way and escape their winter quarters to the welcoming harbors on Lake Michigan. The river bridges go up, and the road traffic above the river has to stop and wait.

A century and a half ago the river was a major commercial waterway, beginning with the completion of the **Illinois and Michigan Canal** in 1848. By 1882, more than 22,000 ships called at the Port of Chicago—more than New York, Philadelphia, Baltimore, Charleston, San Francisco, and Mobile combined. The cost in pollution from ships as well as shore facilities and the subsequent inability of the city to deal with the garbage and waste from a burgeoning population, led to epidemics of cholera and other dread diseases.

Reversing the Flow

In 1889, the Sanitary District of Chicago was created to find a solution to these problems. It revived an earlier plan to reverse the river's flow, to change it from emptying into Lake Michigan to emptying into the Mississippi River system by way of the Des Plaines and Illinois Rivers. On January 16, 1900, the job was accomplished, a feat of engineering some have compared to the building of the Panama Canal. A twenty-eight mile canal had to be built, from which more earth, rocks. etc. were removed than in the Panama project. There were lawsuits from surrounding states, particularly Missouri, who viewed the river reversal as a potential catastrophe. But it was accomplished, and it worked. Chicago's water supply was saved, and the lakefront was preserved to become the thing of beauty it is today.

Fishing for Lunch

The late mayor, Richard J. Daley, envisioned a Chicago River so clean office workers on their lunch hour could drop a hook and catch a lively bass or walleye, then turn it over to a waterfront chef, who would clean and broil it on the spot. It hasn't quite come to that, but the quality of the water is improving, and game fish are doing increasingly well, so it won't be long, one hopes. The riverfront has become fashionable, including restaurants, condominiums, and marinas. Sight seeing and tour boats are commonplace.

Left: The Wrigley Building and Tribune Tower stand at the south end of The Magnificent Mile.

Above: Flowers and plantings of all sorts make North Michigan Avenue a lovely "boulevard."

MICHIGAN AVENUE

North Michigan Avenue

It would be hard to overstate the importance to Chicago of that stretch of North Michigan Avenue, from the Chicago River bridge to Oak Street, known as **The Magnificent Mile**. The large segment

of the American population which derives great recreational pleasure from the act of *shopping* , finds this is the place to be. Three vertical malls, each more magnificent than the other, provide scores of shops, stores, boutiques, and restaurants, from fast food to elegant cuisine—all just an elevator or

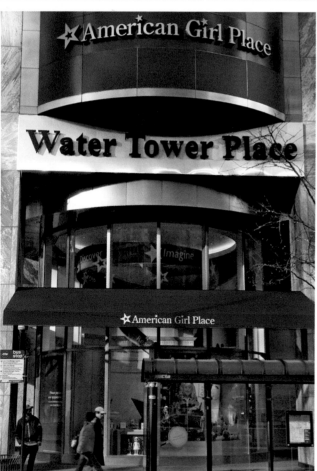

Above: Crate & Barrel Building, 646 N. Michigan.

Left: Water Tower Place with the immensely popular American Girl Place.

escalator ride one from the other. Serious shopping begins on the south end at a new Nordstrom's and ends in a blaze of trendy world class clothing boutiques just around the corner on Oak Street. In between: Fields, Neiman-Marcus, Bloomingdale, Saks.

...and more Michigan Avenue

The addition of the **Crate & Barrel Building** has brightened up the Boulevard. It's across the street from **Nike Town** where one can scope the various offerings of that popular brand. **Chicago Place and Water Tower Place** are vertical malls, offering in a variety of shops just about every kind of merchandise. **The John Hancock Center** offers a delightful plaza, for browsing, *alfresco* dining, and just resting between shopping attacks.

Above: Water Tower Place, 845 N. Michigan.

Right top: John Hancock Plaza, 875 N. Michigan.

Right bottom: Nike Town Chicago, 669 N. Michigan.

Below: Inside Water Tower Place.

Left: Chicago Water Tower.

Above: Horse drawn carriages at the Water Tower.

THE WATER TOWER—SYMBOL OF SURVIVAL

When, in 1871, the City of Chicago burned for three days, a dazed citizenry turned northward to see that the "castellated Gothic style" **Chicago Water Tower** was still standing. The limestone, quarried in nearby Lemont, resisted the blaze, which was by then dying down a mile north of the river and three miles north of Mrs. O'Leary's barn. Inevitably, the story of the Water Tower is bound into the story of the **Great Chicago Fire**. More than 100,000 people were left homeless as a third of the city's residences were destroyed.

The 154 foot Tower, designed by William W. Boyington and built in 1869, was really a decorated standpipe (removed in 1911) which stabilized the pressure of water that moved through the **Pumping Station** across the street at 163 East Pearson. The other building, though in the same style and of the same limestone, is lower and less visually arresting. Yet it's the place that houses the heavy machinery that does the work to this day. This building stands at the end of a tunnel projecting two miles out into Lake Michigan—far enough, in 1871, to reach beyond the pollution that plagued the city's shoreline and to deliver clean water to the growing population. Today the recently renamed **Chicago Water Works** serves more than 300,000 people in Chicago's downtown area.

A major tourist attraction

Today, it is the modest pumping station building that draws the crowds. It holds one of the city's **Visitor Information Centers**, where tourists can get free brochures, maps, and event schedules as well as informed advice and answers to questions.

Above: The north end of the Mag Mile where the greatest concentration of retail stores is located.

Left: Water Tower; Water Tower Place; Hancock Building—three famous landmarks that say, "Chicago."

Right: The south end of the Mag Mile has the hotels and office buildings and some great stores.

Below: The Chicago Water Works, architectural companion to the Water Tower.

Above: Streeterville seen from the Lincoln Park Lagoon.

Right: Streeterville seen from the north end of Oak Street Beach.

THE JOHN HANCOCK CENTER NEIGHBORHOOD

Streeterville was named for a rascal, Cap Streeter, who sailed into Chicago in 1885 and ran his leaky ship aground on a sand bar about where the **John Hancock Center** stands today. After several weeks, unable to free his boat, Streeter built a causeway to the nearby land which was being developed as a "Gold Coast" residential district. He encouraged builders to dump their earth, sand, and gravel (from excavations) around his stranded boat. They did so, and *voilà*, a landfill.

Cap Streeter checked his maps and his lawbooks and declared his new territory to be not a part of the State of Illinois. He called it "Streeterville" and claimed allegiance only to the federal government. He sold lots for as little as $1 each to his drinking buddies and others seeking a promising return on land speculation. He also developed a brisk bootleg booze business. Not until 1918, imagine!, did the government nail Cap for income tax evasion (foreshadowing the Al Capone "solution" many years later) and also for selling whiskey illegally on Sunday.

Say what you will, it was a pretty good 33-year living for one of Chicago's truly unique characters.

Today, Streeterville includes everything east of Michigan Avenue from the river mouth north to Oak Street. That includes the stretch of Lake Shore Drive which runs east to west as the Lake Michigan shore bends at Oak Street Beach—the real Gold Coast. Oh, there are those who will tell you the Gold Coast extends farther north on Lake Shore Drive to North Avenue. Don't believe them.

The south end of Streeterville includes **Navy Pier** and the massive **Norhwestern Hospital** complex. The north end is dominated by **Water Tower Place**, the country's most successful vertical mall, and the **John Hancock Center**, Chicago's third tallest building—a landmark in every way. Architect Bruce Graham of Skidmore Owings & Merril and engineer Fazlur Kahn designed the building wider at the base than at the top, with visible X-shaped cross bracing.

Above: All year round Navy Pier has many attractions for visitors.

Left: Navy Pier.

Following two pages: Navy Pier as seen from the balloon, that takes passengers high up for an interesting aerial view.

NAVY PIER

Navy Pier—newest old jewel in Chicago's crown

Back in 1916, Municipal Pier No. 2 was built 3,000 feet into the lake. As part of the Burnham Plan, it was to receive freight vessels and excursion ships and to be a place for public recreation, with its own streetcar line from the central city. It never quite got there. Shipping was diverted to better facilities at Calumet Harbor, and in World War II, the U.S. Navy took it over as a training facility; hence the name. The pier served as the University of Illinois' Chicago Campus ("Harvard on the rocks") after the war and enjoyed several partial renovations but no clear sense of direction. Then in 1989 the Metropolitan Pier & Exposition Authority received $150 million to begin conversion to a modern recreational and cultural facility.

In 1995, Navy Pier finally opened as Daniel Burnham might have envisioned it. Concerts, sightseeing boats, casual and gourmet restaurants, and much more greet visitors. A giant Ferris Wheel is illuminated at night and is visible from anywhere on Lake Shore Drive. By day, look for the graceful **Lake Point Tower** apartment building which stands alone at the Pier's entrance.

The **Chicago Children's Museum** is a favorite attraction for locals and visitors alike. Mimes and street musicians dot the pier in summer. The **Festival Hall Convention Center** offers 165,000 sq. ft. of exhibition space. Chicago's **Shakespeare Theater** wins awards and sends productions to England! The six-story white theater building is about midway out on the Pier.

There's a congenial **Beer Garden**—a conservatory called **Crystal Gardens**, a six story glass building filled with exotic plants— a movie theater— an ice skating rink in winter.
The original charming **Ballroom** at the east end has been preserved and still hosts smaller events, and the deck outside is a vantage point for truly spectacular views of the city.

MILLENNIUM PARK

LOOKING FORWARD TO A GREATER CENTURY FOR CHICAGO

Since the Great Chicago Fire destroyed much of the city in 1871, a spirit of "I will," has prevailed here. Building and rebuilding Chicago never stops. From the graceful Doric-style columns to the four concealed photocell stations that provide solar power to produce electricity, **Millennium Park** brings the future into the present while honoring the past. Generous private and business donors are named throughout the park. Civic leaders and business donors: Pritzker, Crown, Harris, Wrigley, and Lurie, SBC, BP, Excelon, and Chicago Tribune.

The BP Bridge...a pedestrian walkway of stainless steel panels that's fun to travel. Children love its banks and curves. It shields concert audiences from traffic noise. Designed by Frank Gehry as a companion piece to the music pavilion.

PRITZKER MUSIC PAVILION

Architect Frank Gehry's unique design features a billowing cluster of stainless steel "petals" jutting 120 feet into the sky. It frames the concert stage, connects to a trellis of tubing which supports an array of speakers, and provides the most natural outdoor sound. 4,000 seats and lawn space for 7,000 lie beneath this acoustical canopy. Concerts are frequent and free.

Michigan Avenue

Monroe Street

Randolph Street

The Crown Fountain

South Terrace

Chase Promenade South

Nichols Bridgeway

Exelon Pavilion
Millennium Garage

The Lurie Garden

Exelon Pavilion
Millennium Garage

McCormick Tribune Plaza and Ice Rink

Grant Park North Garage

Park Grill Restaurant

Cloud Gate (Sculpture)

Chase Promenade Central

AT&T Plaza

Great Lawn

Wrigley Square

North Terrace

Chase Promenade North

Exelon Pavilion Welcome Center

Roof Terrace

Jay Pritzker Pavilion

Harris Theater for Music and Dance

Exelon Pavilion
Millennium Garage

BP Bridge

Bike Station

Columbus Drive

Millennium Park - The great lawn in front of the spectacular Pritzker Music Pavilion where 11,000 listeners may enjoy a summer concert.

N⟶

"CLOUD GATE"
POPULAR SCULPTURE
ON THE SBC PLAZA

British sculptor Anish Kapoor created this 110 ton polished stainless steel work as an "interactive" sculpture where visitors are encouraged to walk around and beneath it...which they do in droves. Affectionately nicknamed "**The Bean**," Cloud Gate is one of Millennium Park's most popular attractions, especially for photographers.

The Crown Fountain, an instant magnet for all pre-teen children, has two 50 foot towers made of glass blocks at either end of a shallow reflecting pool. Water cascades from the tops of the towers over huge faces that change expressions; new faces appear; and now and then water squirts from giant mouths. Spanish sculptor Jaume Plensa dreamed this one up, and what a hit it is!

Top: Clean and tidy, the comfortable row-seats of the music pavilion await an audience. Top right: colored lights play on the steel panels and on the stage during a winter light show.

Middle: A 16,000 sq. ft. ice skating rink at Washington Street and Michigan Avenue offers skate rental, a warm lobby, and public lockers. There's an adjoining restaurant, the Park Grill, which expands into the skating area in summertime.

Bottom: Wrigley Square at the corner of Michigan and Randolph offers a quiet, contemplative lawn for strolling or relaxing. The names of donors - both individual and corporate - are etched in stone at the base of the columned monument.

Top: The intriguing entrance to the 1500 seat Harris Theater for music and dance, is on Randolph Street, but the theater itself descends five stories underground where ample parking is available.

Top right: Cloud Gate ("the Bean") is easily viewed from offices across Michigan Avenue. The snow on top creates a huge sugar donut.

Right and below: The Lurie Garden includes both large and surprisingly intimate spaces and displays shrubs, trees, and flowers... hundreds of varieties, most of which are grown in the Lurie's own outdoor plant nursery.

Millennium Park has extended Grant Park northwards, while the Art Institute in Grant Park added an extension, with the Modern Wing, at its north-east corner. Both are connected by the Nichols Bridgeway.

The stunning Buckingham Fountain shows best against the city's night sky.

GRANT PARK

Grant Park is Chicago's most celebrated public space. In 1835 it was the first area to be designated as public land extending from Randolph Street in the north to 11th Street in the south between Michigan Ave and the lake. Since 1927 the heart of Grant Park has been **Buckingham Fountain**, yet on both ends the park has been a work in progress. Through lane changes of Lakeshore Drive, surface parking and railroad tracks put underground, landscaping the

Museum Campus, creation of the Millennium Park Extension, Grant Park is now a beautiful and huge playground that suits every taste: world famous museums, public art, outdoor concerts, large venue performances (Lollapalooza), large outdoor festivals (Blues, Jazz, Gospel, Taste), recreational fields and happenings (Marathon), important gatherings for the Chicagoans (President Obama's election night, the Dalhi Lama, the Pope).

Above: The Art Institute on Michigan Avenue, opened in 1894.

Facing top right: The Fountain of the Great Lakes by Lorado Taft, 1913.

Facing top left: A Chicago symbol the world over.

Facing bottom: A Sunday on La Grande Jatte, by George Seurat, oil on canvas. 1884.

THE ART INSTITUTE

One of the World's Leading Museums

The Art Institute of Chicago lets you discover forty centuries of creativity, from ancient Chinese bronzes to the latest work of today's artists. There are Rembrandts, African wood carvings, suits of armor, ancient weapons, sculptures, prints, drawings, photographs, and miniature rooms of great beauty.

The internationally acclaimed collection of Impressionist and post- Impressionist painters includes outstanding works by Monet, Renoir, Degas, and Van Gogh, among others. Possibly the most viewed pictures in the Art Institute are Georges Seurat's *A Sunday on La Grand Jatte—1884* , Mary Cassatt's *The Bath,* and Grant Wood's celebrated *American Gothic.*
The building is a large one, and, unless time is unlimited, it is a good idea to ask an Institute guide for directions to areas of special interest.
Galleries of Chinese, Japanese, and Korean art have been opened recently, and the Thorne Rooms remain a favorite destination for visitors. Sixty-eight European and American Rooms are reproduced in miniature, tracing the history of interior design.

The Art Institute is open seven days a week except on Thanksgiving, Christmas and New Year's days.

The Art Institute has two restaurants, - *Terzo Piano* in the Modern Wing and the *Garden Café* with a summer courtyard on the lower level of the original building.
There is a *Museum Shop* filled with art books, reproductions, postcards, slides, jewelry, and unusual gifts, all for sale.

The Modern Wing of the Art Institute

The **Modern Wing** opened in 2009 and with its added space makes the Art Institute the second largest museum in the country. It is dedicated to the collections of European Modern Art, Contemporary Art, Architecture and Design, Prints and Drawings and Special Exhibitions. Permanent and temporary exhibitions are shown on three floors in a building that incorporates design, technology and green architecture. On the first floor, the expanded **Ryan Education Center** hosts programs for families, groups, teachers, and teens.

Award winning architect Renzo Piano is giving the Art Institute a new look: a street level garden can be seen from a two-story glass staircase, integrating nature with the art spaces. A sunroof (named "flying carpet") hovers over the wing and provides ideal light conditions while minimizing energy needs.
A bold **footbridge Nichols Bridgeway** connects the Modern Wing to **Millennium Park**.

Facing top: Art lovers in the galleries of the European Modern Collections in the Modern Wing.

Below: The Modern Wing by Renzo Piano, the newest addition to the Art Institute.

Facing bottom: View of the Modern Wing from the Lurie Garden in Millennium Park.

The ever changing steps of the Museum of Contemporary Art (MCA) are in character with the museum's mission.
Bottom left: Chicago Historical Society in Lincoln Park.
Bottom right: Chicago Cultural Center at Michigan Ave across from Millennium Park.

MUSEUM OF CONTEMPORARY ART

Chicago's **Museum of Contemporary Art** is the youngest member of the local fine arts family, founded in 1967 and occupying its present building since 1996. The **MCA** is commited to exhibiting art of the present. It is a laboratory—experimenting, informing and illuminating the nature of contemporary art. Located just east of the famous **Water Tower**, the museum presents a wide range of visual and performance art by established artists: Duchamp, Ernst, Miró, Dubuffet, and Warhol as well as cutting edge work by Paschke, Golub, and Nutt. A terraced outdoor sculpture garden faces Lake Michigan to the east.

CHICAGO HISTORICAL SOCIETY

People interested in Chicago *per se*, its history and culture, will enjoy the **Chicago Historical Society** at 1601 Clark Street at North Avenue. There are fascinating collections of period costumes, photographs and prints, decorative arts, manuscripts, paintings and sculpture. Lincoln is treated extensively as are Illinois' native American cultures. Temporary exhibitions are ingenious and frequently changing, and the Society sponsors many programs and excursions for both adults and children.

CHICAGO CULTURAL CENTER

Originally designed as a neo-classic palace and as a public library to house the large book donation from England after the Great Fire, it was to be a "monument worthy of a great and public spirited city." Today, as home of the **Chicago Cultural Center**, the building fulfills that dictum. Programs are free and are of the highest standard: art and photography exhibitions, films, theater, music and lectures. CCC concerts and programs are presented against a splendid background of interior surfaces clad in mosaics and marble that rise to a monumental Tiffany stained glass dome in Preston Bradly Hall.

The CCC is also home to the city's **Visitor Information Center**.

Museum Campus showing the Shedd Aquarium and Field Museum.

MUSEUM CAMPUS

In 1995, the Chicago Park District took the radical step of relocating Lake Shore Drive west of **Soldier Field** and the **Field Museum**. An extension of **Burnham Park** was created to provide a traffic-free "campus," replete with landscaped walkways and very convenient parking for thousands of cars. Now three of the most famous Chicago attractions are uniquely linked on this corner of land jutting into Lake Michigan between **Monroe Harbor** and **Burnham Harbor**.

Visitors can take in the **Field Museum of Natural History**, the **John G. Shedd Aquarium**, and the **Adler Planetarium** and make a leisurely day of it. Food, rest rooms, CTA Bus transportation—all are available, and everything is handicap-accessible. A free Museum Campus Trolley runs continuously. Other Chicago institutions of equal stature—the **Art Institute** and **The Museum of Science and Industry**, for examples—share the characteristics of generous parking availability and accessibility, but no single site offers the diversity of the new **Museum Campus**.

Soldier Field, located just to the south and part of the campus, is the home of professional football's **Chicago Bears**. This venerable stadium has been renovated and is now the very model of a modern professional sports facility.

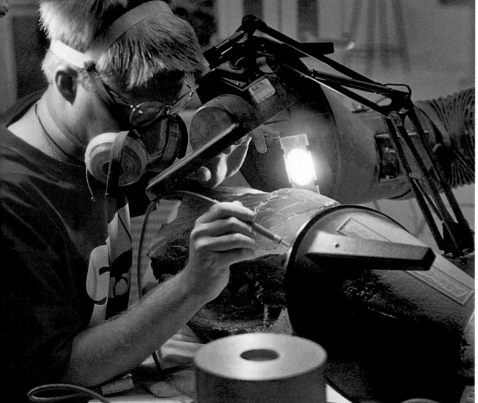

The Greek temple-inspired building of the Field Museum of Natural History.

Facing page: The beautiful Shedd Aquarium at sunrise.

Left: The MacDonald's Fossil Preparation Laboratory is open to public view.

FIELD MUSEUM OF NATURAL HISTORY

Explore an Egyptian tomb. Unwrap the secrets of ancient mummies. Enter this classic Greek Revival building and pass *underneath* the skeleton of the world's largest dinosaur displayed anywhere. It's a Brachiosaurus: 75 ft. long and 40 ft. tall. Back in Colorado in the later Jurassic period (150 million years ago), this fellow probably weighed 50 to 80 tons. See a wooly mammoth and stuffed animals of all kinds shown in natural settings. It's a naturalist's feast for young and old alike.

Top: the Oceanarium.

Left: The main entrance to the Shedd Aquarium is flanked by the Man with Fish Garden.

SHEDD AQUARIUM

This has become a "hot" tourist attraction since 1991, when it became the largest aquarium in the world. The addition of a new **Oceanarium** is home to dolphins, seals, otters, penguins, and even Beluga whales. Five times daily these marine mammals frolic for the public. The original building, designed to blend with the Field Museum, features a 900,000 gallon coral reef containing an enormous variety of tropical fish, as well as sea turtles, sharks, and green moray eels. Free admission on Thursdays.

The Adler Planetarium lies to the east on a peninsula which is part of the Museum Campus, taking in the sun, moon and stars from all four directions.

Right: The Star Rider virtual reality experience.

ADLER PLANETARIUM

A new **Sky Pavilion** helps this venerable attraction keep up with its neighbors. The Planetarium presentations can transport visitors to planets, comets, stars, and galaxies far from Earth. Three floors of exhibits and dazzling sky shows help unlock the cosmic secrets. The technology is cutting-edge enough to satisfy the most enthusiastic computer-oriented youngster, yet not too alarming for comfort-oriented adults. Truly, it's a great show.

Above: Interactive Exhibits at the Adler Planetarium. There are numerous exhibits which can be activated by visitors, many of them particularly interesting to children.

Right: Henry Moore sculpture—a 13 foot sundial—fronts the Planetarium. Other Moore works may be found at the University of Chicago and at Northwestern University.

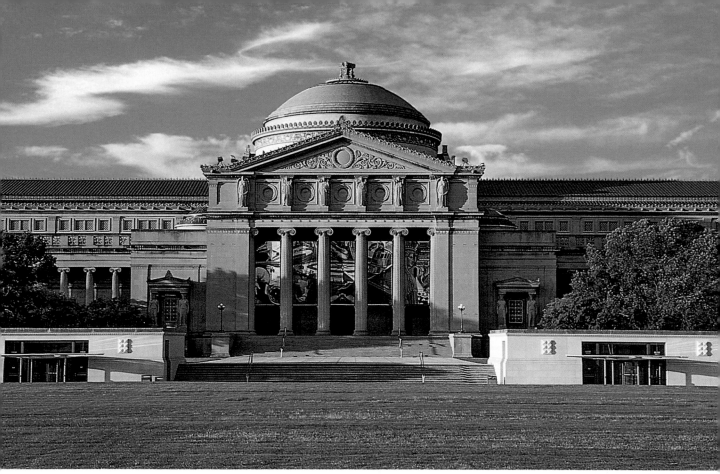

Above: The Museum of Science and Industry.

Right: Neo-classical Greek adornment.

HYDE PARK

Until almost 1890, Hyde Park was an affluent southern suburb of Chicago, founded in 1852 to be industry-free, the residential equivalent of Lake Forest, north of the city. But Chicago grew so rapidly to the south that annexation could no longer be resisted in 1889. In 1891, the neighborhood was chosen as the site of the **World's Columbian Exposition**. About the same time, John D. Rockefeller's **University of Chicago** was established in Hyde Park. Today, it is an island of tree-lined stability in a south side of changing social and ethnic patterns.

Above: Museum of Science and Industry viewed from the south.

MUSEUM OF SCIENCE AND INDUSTRY

The only building erected for the 1893 Columbian Exposition still standing, this neo-classical masterpiece, designed by Daniel Burnham, has been reconstructed, added-to, and redesigned frequently over the century. It stands today as one of Chicago's top tourist attractions.

After the Columbian Exposition ended the "Palace of Fine Arts" became the Field Museum and remained such until the Field moved north in 1920.

The grand (but crumbling) old building stood empty in Jackson Park until, in 1926, Julius Rosenwald, millionaire chairman of Sears Roebuck, took an interest. He had seen an industrial museum in Munich, Germany, and he eventually donated more than $7 million to a restoration which took until 1940 to complete. The **Coal Mine** was the main attraction in those early days with its simulated elevator shaft, bituminous walls, and rickety rail cars. It was *very* realistic. Today's exhibits are high tech, of course, but the same scientific accuracy and attention to detail prevail.

Nowadays visitors can **Take Flight** (simulated) in a Boeing 727 jet—visit the **Coal Mine** or a **Submarine**—walk through 16-foot **Heart** replica—stroll down **Yesterday's Main Street** and check out a silent movie. The variety of exhibits seems endless.

Above: Colleen Moore's Fairy Castle dollhouses, furnished with more than a thousand miniature treasures.

Below: Apollo 8 Overview—features the command module, the first vessel ever to circle the moon, in 1968. There is also a "space shuttle" in which visitors can experience the sensation of liftoff and space travel.

Above: DuSable Museum in Washington Park.

Facing page top: Ida Noyes Hall Student Center on the Midway Plaisance.

Facing page bottom: Rockefeller Chapel.

DUSABLE MUSEUM

This building lies in Washington Park, a stone's throw across Cottage Grove Avenue, the western boundary of Hyde Park. Exhibits trace the life of Chicago's first permanent non-native settler. Jean Baptiste Pont du Sable arrived at the Checagou portage before 1790. He was a black man—a successful trader from the Caribbean island of Hispaniola. A permanent exhibit, **Up From Slavery**, shows the development of slavery in this country. There are traveling exhibits as well and many interesting African American memorabilia.

MIDWAY PLAISANCE

This broad boulevard runs next to 59th Street and connects Washington Park to Jackson Park, forming the south boundary of the **Hyde Park** neighborhood. It was created to hold the Ferris Wheel and various other amusements for the 1893 World's Fair. The frolicsome atmosphere gave rise to subsequent use of the word "midway" to descibe carnivals the world over. Interesting sculptures stand at each end: **Fountain of Time** by Lorado Taft on the west—and the **Thomas Masaryk Memorial** on the east honoring the father of Czechoslovakia, a huge mounted knight in full armor: Saint Wenceslaus.

ROCKEFELLER CHAPEL

Viewed from the Midway, this massive Gothic limestone church reminds one that the Rockefeller family and the University took religion very seriously. **Rockefeller Chapel** is intended "to remove the mind of the student from the busy mercantile condition of Chicago and surround him with the peculiar air of quiet dignity." In addition to Episcopal services, the chapel offers frequent organ and carillon recitals and programs of choral music.

FRANK LLOYD WRIGHT'S ROBIE HOUSE

Just north of Rockefeller Chapel and across Woodlawn Avenue stands the showpiece dwelling many critics feel represents the finest of Frank Lloyd Wright's Prairie School houses. Designed for successful bicycle manufacturer Frederick C. Robie, the house consists of parallel rectangular two-story masses, at the meeting of which rises a smaller, square third story. The house almost seems to float. This particular design is the one that made Wright famous and helped architecture break away from the constraints of tradition. The interior is open, embelished by Wright-designed furniture and exquisite leaded and stained glass doors and windows. A guided tour is available daily at noon.

Left and below: Robie House in Hyde Park is considered by many to be Frank Lloyd Wright's masterpiece.

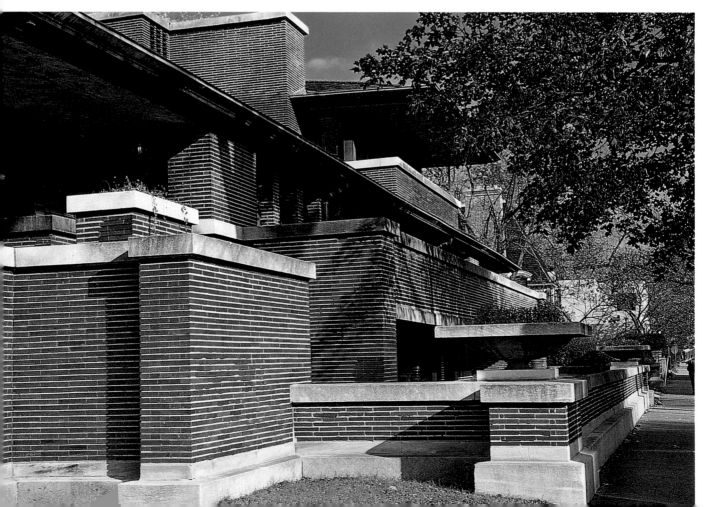

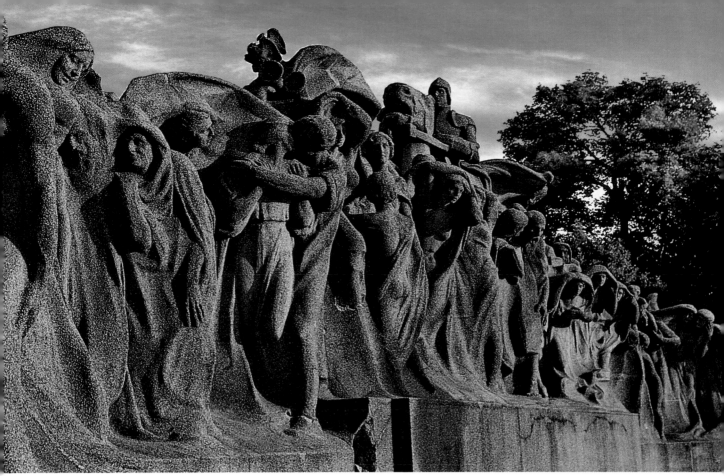

Above: Lorado Taft's Fountain of Time, 1922.

Right: Henry Moore's "Nuclear Energy", 1967.

FOUNTAIN OF TIME

This massive (110 foot) wave of humanity stands at the western end of the Midway Plaisance. "Time," the lonely sentinel, stands across a pool of water from one hundred individual figures—soldiers, refugees, lovers, youngsters, oldsters, and includes the sculptor himself, Lorado Taft, and his assistants. **Fountain of Time** was cast in a mold made of 4,500 pieces, formed of what was then, in 1922, a new material: steel-reinforced hollow-cast concrete, which was supposed to stand the test of time. Sadly, it has not, and the surface of the sculpture is in appalling condition due to the stresses of weather and air pollution. So far, the money that would be necessary to restore it has not been found.

"NUCLEAR ENERGY"

Set on the very spot where Enrico Fermi and his team devised the first nuclear reactor is this massive twelve-foot bronze, Moore's imposing work suggests at once a protective helmet, a human skull, and a mushroom-shaped cloud.

UNIVERSITY OF CHICAGO CAMPUS

One of America's finest universities is located in Hyde Park, a south side neighborhood with sharply defined borders: Cottage Grove Avenue on the west to the Lake—and Hyde Park Blvd. (51st Street) on the north to the Midway Plaisance. Founded with generous funding from John D. Rockefeller in the 1890s, the **University of Chicago** has produced more Nobel Prize winners than any other university. Many of the prizes came in Economics, a field in which the "Chicago School" is well known.

The architect, Henry Ives Cobb, planned the campus as six broken quadrangles of strictly Gothic buildings, constructed on land donated by Marshall Field. Cobb was much influenced by the University trustees who felt Gothic had ecclesiastical and educational traditions which made it a more appropriate style for a university than Romanesque, which was high fashion in the 1890s. What followed was a forty-year Gothic building spree and a campus which is *not* made for automobiles: one has to walk the quadrangles. They're very beautiful, very traditional, with a fine selection of outdoor sculptures. A few post WW II buildings nearby break the Gothic mode.

Three views of the University of Chicago Campus.

OAK PARK

For those interested in the work of Frank Lloyd Wright, the Village of **Oak Park**, west of Chicago, is a treasure trove beyond imagining. The village was settled in the years following the Chicago Fire of 1871. It was an island of purity, free from alcohol, immigrants, and other "bringers of moral decay." It was established as an independent village in 1902. It was home not only to Wright but to authors Ernest Hemingway and Edgar Rice Burroughs, creator of the "Tarzan" books. Today, Oak Park is economically stable, integrated and progressive; home to well-educated leaders of the Chicagoland community.

For the Frank Lloyd Wright *aficionados*, everything is well organized; many guided tours are available. The best place to begin is the **Visitors Center** at 158 N. Forest Avenue. It is open every day from 10 to 5 (4 p.m. in winter) and provides orientation, maps, guidebooks, and gift items. Of more than 270 houses created by Wright, 26 are located in Oak Park and adjacent River Forest. In addition, the **Unity Temple**, one of his most famous buildings, is located just a block east of the Visitors Center.

Frank Lloyd Wright's Home and Studio

Wright's **Home and Studio** was begun in 1889. Here, Wright lived and worked for twenty years, raised six children with his first wife, Catherine Tobin, and established what is known as the "Prairie School" of architecture.

The house was completed in 1895 with the addition of a dining room and a kitchen/playroom. The studio addition went up in 1898. It showcases Wright's love of geometric shapes. After Wright left Oak Park, he remodeled the studio as living quarters for the family.
Later the buildings were remodeled into six apartments and rented out. In 1974, the complex was acquired by the National Trust for Historic

Below: Frank Lloyd Wright's home and studio in Oak Park.

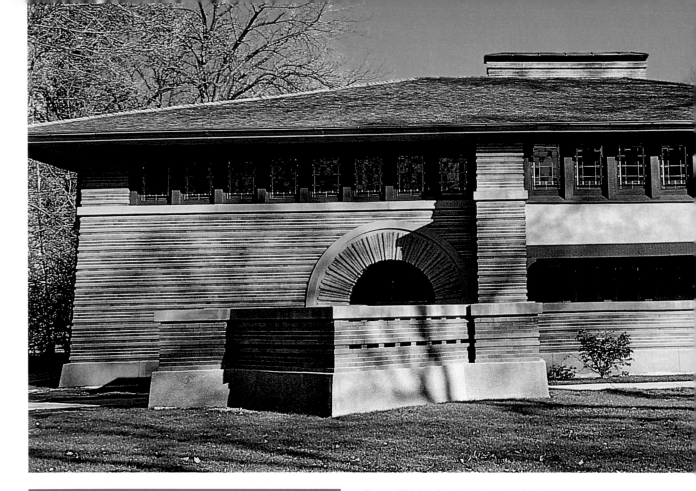

Above: Wright's Heurtley House in Oak Park.

Left: Wrights Unity Temple in Oak Park.

Preservation and restored by the Frank Lloyd Wright Home and Studio Foundation to its 1905-09 appearance.

Frank Lloyd Wright arrived in Chicago in 1886 from rural Wisconsin when he was nineteen, the child of a "progressive" mother and a musician father. He apprenticed first with J.L. Silsbee, primarily a house designer, and then was hired as a draftsman by the firm of Adler and Sullivan. Louis Sullivan, probably the most famous architect of his time,`` became Wright's mentor and collaborator on several landmark designs. Wright worked on the design for Chicago's **Auditorium building**, designed by Sullivan. He opened his own office in 1893 and continued to work and experiment for 66 years until his death in 1959.

Heurtley House

The **Heurtley House** at 318 N. Forest Avenue is one of Wright's most magnificent homes. The living rooms are raised to enable the occupants to see out through uncurtained art glass windows and are situated high enough so outsiders cannot see inside the house.

Unity Temple

The **Unity Temple** at 875 Lake Street is not large. Rather it is a sequence of intimate spaces designed for four hundred church members. Two main blocks form a temple for worship and a "Unity House" for social service functions. High walls and side entrances create a privacy in the stunning interior, where no seat is more than 45 feet from the pulpit.

Thomas House

The **Thomas House** at 210 N. Forest Avenue is thought to be Wright's first constructed Prairie School House. He eliminates the attic and the basement and lavishes his genius on the spaces where people live.

Moore House

The **Moore House** at 333 N. Forest Avenue is, according to the Oak Park Visitors Bureau, "the most widely recognized Frank Lloyd Wright designed home in the world." It was his first commission, in 1905, after leaving the offices of Adler and Sullivan. Interestingly, this Tudor Revival design couldn't be much farther removed from Wright's later signature Prairie Style.

Below left: Wright's Thomas House in Oak Park.

Below: Wright's Moore House in Oak Park.

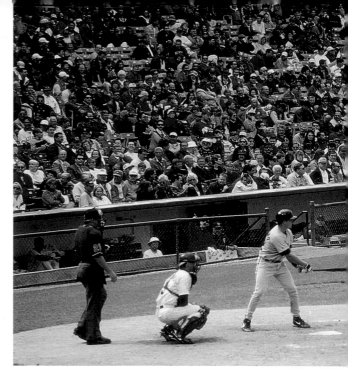

Top: Batter Up at the "Friendly Confines" of Wrigley Field.
Left top: Cubs Park on game day—a neighborhood tradition.
Bottom: As seen from the press box.

CHICAGO SPORTS ARENAS

WRIGLEY FIELD—CUBS PARK

Thirty-six blocks north of Madison Street at the corner of Clark and Addison, **Wrigley Field** began life in 1914 as "Weeghman Field," home of the *Chicago Whales* of the Federal League. Two years later the Cubs moved in, and, unlike almost every other major league team, stayed put. The old ballyard eventually got a row of luxury boxes sandwiched between the upper and lower decks; and, after years of promoting the virtues of day baseball, lights were finally installed and now some games are played at night. That took some doing, because Wrigleyville is very much a *neighborhood*. People live here, and it's also a party area for young folks—lots of music bars, restaurants, and the like. Wrigley Field is *not* surrounded by parking lots like every other sports stadium. Parking is handled by hundreds of small local entrepreneurs, and it works out pretty well. Most fans take the CTA train to the Addison Streeet Station.

U. S. CELLULAR FIELD—WHITE SOX PARK

Built in 1991, this new ballpark is the very model of a modern major league stadium. It seats 43,000, with eighty-four skyboxes, extra-wide walkways, clubs, restaurants, and souvenir shops. Parking is easy. Ramps are gently graded. Lots of restrooms. Wheelchair accessible. In other words, it's almost too nice; it lacks soul. But that's okay, the team is frequently competitive, and the ballpark is still a pleasant place to spend a summer afternoon or evening.

U. S. Cellular Field is particularly easy to reach. Just head south on the Dan Ryan Expressway, and get off at 35th street.

Bottom: The new home of the Chicago White Sox.

UNITED CENTER

Bulls and Blackhawks

One might easily dub this grand new building "the house that Michael built." The years from 1984 to 1998 when Michael Jordan led the Chicago Bulls to six National Basketball Association Championships are warm in the memories of Chicagoans. The skinny North Carolinian with the big ears so dominated the game, we may never see his like again. Sigh. Still the Bulls battle on and on off nights, management floods the rink that lies beneath the hardwood floor, and the Chicago Blackhawks hockey team, another proud big league sports tradition, takes the ice.

Left: Statue of Michael "Air" Jordan at the United Center.

Below: The Chicago Bulls play to capacity crowds.

SOLDIER FIELD

The Chicago Bears

After many years of private and civic effort, Chicago's professional football team has a spectacular new home. A modern asymmetrical 61,000 seat bowl sits within the old Grecian colonnades of the original stadium. Thus, the Bears have the most modern fan-friendly facility. Yet the doughboy soldiers of World War I are still remembered appropiately. It's an odd but striking architectural marriage; and the surrounding grounds are lovely. There is plenty of parking, and it's easy to find, just south of Grant Park on Lake Shore Drive.

Right: The United Center is a prominent building west of the Loop.

Below: Soldier Field, home of the Bears, overlooking Burnham Harbor.

LINCOLN PARK

This is Chicago's largest park and probably the most diversified in the amusements it provides. Miles of beaches. Two large yacht harbors. A world class zoo. Playing fields and facilties for baseball, cycling, softball, soccer, tennis, golf, volleyball, and rowing. And a wonderful collection of public sculpture, including **"The Standing Lincoln,"** by Augustus Saint-Gaudens, erected in 1887, and considered by many sculptors to be the best likeness of our sixteenth president and one of the finest works of monument art in the country. It may be found standing in front of the **Chicago History Museum** building at North Avenue and Clark Street. Also, see the **Ulysses S. Grant Memorial,** a large equestrian statue visible from Lake Shore Drive; and **William Shakespeare**, set in a small quiet garden across from the **Lincoln Park Conservatory**.

Left: Lincoln Park with Belmont Harbor.
Below: Lincoln Park Zoo—open 7 days a week and free for all.

Above: A green Chicago River is a St. Patrick's Day tradition.

Above left: Taste of Chicago in Grant Park delights and over-feeds thousands of hungry locals and visitors.

Below left: The Printers Row Book Fair attracts bargain hunters to the south Loop.

SPECIAL EVENTS AND FAIRS

Nothing in Chicago quite equals of **"Taste of Chicago,"** with its teeming masses of hungry families and cool teenagers "hanging out." **Taste** ends with a spectacular patriotic concert by the **Grant Park Symphony Orchestra** on the evening of July 3. The *1812 Overture* is traditionally played with spectacular fireworks exploding over the lake. But many other events are celebrated as well. All the big ethnic "days" have their parades, some in the Loop, some in neighborhoods. The most spectacular downtown parade is the **St. Patrick's Day Parade**, down Dearborn Street in the Loop in March. Bands, politicians—especially those *currently running for office*, floats, bagpipes, and, yes, the city does dye the river green—very green. Politically, Chicago is still an Irish town.

Art Festivals are popular. Quite good ones may be found in surrounding suburbs almost every weekend in summer.

The locals focus on the traditional art street fairs, beginning in early June with the **57th Street Art Fair**, Chicago's oldest juried fair. It's on the University of Chicago campus in Hyde Park, and it has the low-pressure feel of a neighborhood event, which, of course, it is!

One week later, the popular **Old Town Art Fair** presents many of the same artists in a neighborhood near Lincoln Park. The **Gold Coast Art Fair** calls itself the "world's largest". It takes place in August in River North. And finally, the **Coyote Festival** holds forth in Bucktown/ Wicker Park (northwest of the Loop) in September. It includes architecture, dance, design, experimental films, literature, murals, performance art, sound, and theater. Something for everyone!

Above right: Polkas, jitterbugs, mambos, and fox trots - anything goes at the dance pavilion.

Below right: The annual Art Chicago.
Art Chicago and other summer showings draw serious collectors.

Below: The Grant Park Symphony Orchestra performs from June to September.

MUSIC FESTIVALS

The city sponsors the largest free jazz extravaganza in the world, the **Chicago Jazz Festival**, presented over a period of several days in late August or September. The event is so large, it supplies simultaneous performances at two or three venues; only the biggest names make it to the big shell. Dyed-in-the-wool jazz fans will appreciate some of the stars of tomorrow (and yesterday) who play the smaller stages.

The **Chicago Blues Festival** in June gets better every year, fed by a strong local pool of Blues talent. Big name international stars usually show up as well. Grant Park also hosts the **Chicago Gospel Festival** and a **Country Music Festival**.

Left top: Petrillo Music Shell in Grant Park.

Left bottom: Koko Taylor Blues Band.

Below: The Jazz Festival attracts top talent.

Up close
at the Jazz Festival.

SUMMER LAKEFRONT ACTIVITIES

A strong, well-funded Park District offers programs for Chicagoans of all ages. More than 30 free public beaches open in mid-June with lifeguards on duty from 9 a.m. till early evening. Eight yacht harbors provide moorings for sail and motor vessels, many of the latter primarily engaged in sport fishing. Coho and chinook salmon, steelheads, and lake trout, are the preferred species. Perch are coming back soon, so they say. Fishermen in boats from Chicago harbors get good results beginning in May and continuing through September.

Lincoln Park is the city's largest and busiest park and offers more variety in facilities and activities than any other. 1,212 acres stretch along six miles of lake shore from North Avenue Beach to Foster Street Beach. Three yacht harbors: **Belmont**, **Diversey**, and **Montrose** are available to boaters, and a very accessible and popular zoo caters mainly to families. In addition to lions and great apes and

Top: 3-man (and 3-woman) basketball teams dominate the summer park scene.

Bottom: Cycling and jogging paths run for many miles through the parks.

Top: Big time beach volleyball has come to North Avenue Beach. Locals play, too.

Middle: Triathlon competitors prove themselves swimming, cycling, and running.

Bottom: The Chicago Marathon is on the world circuit.

Following pages: The annual Chicago to Mackinac Race—world's longest fresh water sailing event.

a large assortment of other large wild animals, there's a **Farm in the Zoo** with all the typical domestic species. There is also a **Petting Zoo** where toddlers can safely put their hands on baby animals, under the careful supervision of zoo handlers. **Lincoln Park** also contains some interesting statuary, a golf course, tennis courts, soccer and baseball fields. The Park District is active in promoting leagues, and programs for team sports abound. Opportunities also exist for individual sports: running, cycling, swimming and the like.

THE RESTAURANT SCENE

Chicago is home to world class restaurants in many parts in the city and suburbs. Most accessible for the visitor is the RIVER NORTH district. Many have heard of the PIZZERIA UNO and DUO and their famous Deep Dish Chicago Style Pizza. For serious ethnic food, one needs to find Greek town and Chinatown. Italian, Thai, Chinese, Mexican and Indian restaurants can be easily discovered everywhere.

Top: Sidewalk cafes proliferate in summer. Middle (3): River North offers great variety in dining. Bottom left: Dining al fresco is increasingly popular. Bottom right: Harry Carey's gone, but his restaurant lives on.

Getting Around

Top: Carriages can always be found near the Water Tower on Michigan Avenue.

Below: CTA Rapid Transit electric trains above and below ground and buses reach all areas of the city.
Fast reliable Metra commuter trains service the suburbs.

THE NORTH SHORE

NORTHWESTERN UNIVERSITY
IN EVANSTON

Adjoining Chicago on the north, the City of
Evanston is home to the beautiful lakefront campus
of **Northwestern University**. Shown at left is a
portion of that campus, built in recent years on land
reclaimed from Lake Michigan. Northwestern is a
member of The Big Ten conference.

BAHA'I HOUSE OF WORSHIP
IN WILMETTE

This lovely reinforced concrete building is nine-
sided, the number nine being highly symbolic in
the Baha'i faith. Delicate, lacy designs rise four
stories over the lakefront in Wilmette, the next
suburb north. The interior is a series of soaring
geometric patterns reaching up into the dome.
Designed by Louis Bourgeois and built in 1953, the
building offers guided tours.

CHICAGO BOTANIC GARDENS
IN GLENCOE

Here are 300 acres full of plants, trees, and flowers;
hills, lakes, and islands, so artfully arranged it's like
another world. Open air bus tours run all day long,
or the gardens can be walked in two or three hours,
with many congenial picnic sites available along the
way. There is an information center complete with gift
shop and indoor plant exhibits.

Outside, a gorgeous rose garden, an extensive
Japanese garden—there is even a carillon with
concerts on summer nights. Open seven days.

Left top: Northwestern University's Evanston campus.

Left bottom: The Baha'i House of Worship and Wilmette Harbor.

Below: Glencoe's Botanic Gardens.

O'HARE INTERNATIONAL AIRPORT

After years of improvisation, Chicago's O'Hare Airport, located on the northwest corner of the city, can now truly be called **O'Hare International**. It competes with Atlanta's airport for the title of "busiest in the world." Yet, for all its largeness, there is demand for yet another airport in Chicago to supplement O'Hare and Midway (a smaller airport on the southwest side of the city). The Illinois General Assembly debates the issue annualy.

In the mid '90s, one of the most ambitious improvement programs ever undertaken by a major airport was completed. There is now a state-of-the-art International Terminal, totally separate from the domestic operation, and an inter-airport Electric Rail Transit System to connect the two. The terminal is vast, spread wide to accomodate the largest jets. Electric carts shuttle passengers to and from departure and arrival gates.

There are 156 ticketing positions on the departure level. Multiple Immigration and Customs stations greet arrivals and speed them through. As air traffic increases in the twenty-first century, O'Hare can still expand to handle additional traffic. Another runway is proposed.

A City Visitor Information Center is staffed with multi-lingual representatives. Fast, inexpensive CTA rail service connects O'Hare to the Loop.

Left: The Grand Concourse in the International Terminal.

Right and below: The north facade and the walkway from parking to the International Terminal.

INDEX